CW00401495

Text: *Harri Roberts*

Series editor: *Tony Bowerman*

Photographs: *Harri Roberts, Tracy Burton, Steve Young Photography, Botond Szabo, Paula J James, Gareth Lovering, Robin Croft, Phil Fitzsimmons, Paul Edwards/Aspects of Wales, Lizzie Wilberforce/ Wildlife Trust of South and West Wales, www.discovercarmarthenshire. com, © Crown copyright (2013) Visit Wales, Shutterstock, Dreamstime, Fotolia*

Design: *Carl Rogers*

ISBN 978-1-908632-16-6

A CIP catalogue record for this book is available from the British Library.

www.northerneyebooks.co.uk

Cover: Rhossili Bay, Gower (Walk 7)
Photo: *Botond Szabo | www.flickr.com/photos/ straighthead*

Important Advice: The routes described in this book are undertaken at the reader's own risk. Walkers should take into account their level of fitness, wear suitable footwear and clothing, and carry food and water. It is also advisable to take the relevant OS map with you in case you get lost and leave the area covered by our maps.

Whilst every care has been taken to ensure the accuracy of the route directions, the publisher cannot accept responsibility for errors or omissions, or for changes in the details given. Nor can the publisher and copyright owners accept responsibility for any consequences arising from the use of this book.

If you find any inaccuracies in either the text or maps, please either write to us or email us at the addresses below. Thank you.

First published in 2013 by:

Northern Eye Books Limited
Northern Eye Books, Tattenhall, Cheshire CH3 9PX

This edition published 2018.

Email: tony@northerneyebooks.com

For sales enquiries, please call 01928 723 744

www.walescoastpath.co.uk
www.northerneyebooks.co.uk
www.top10walks.co.uk

 Twitter: @HarriRoberts7
@WalesCoastUK
@Northerneyeboo

Contents

The **Wales Coast Path**

Wales is the only country in the world with a path around its entire coast. The long-distance **Wales Coast Path** offers 870 miles/1440 kilometres of unbroken coastal walking, from the outskirts of the walled city of Chester in the north to the market town of Chepstow in the south.

There's something new around every corner. Visually stunning and rich in both history and wildlife, the path promises ever-changing views, wildflowers and seabirds, as well as castles, coves and coastal pubs. In fact, the Wales Coast Path runs through 1 Marine Nature Reserve, 2 National Parks, 3 Areas of Outstanding Natural Beauty, 11 National Nature Reserves, 14 Heritage Coasts, and 23 Historic Landscapes. And, to cap it all, the **Wales Coast Path** links up with the long-distance Offa's Dyke path at either end: creating a complete, 1,030 mile circuit of the whole of Wales.

Gower's iconic Rhossili beach is backed by Rhossili Down.

Carmarthen Bay & the Gower Peninsula

Carmarthen Bay embraces an area of Welsh coast stretching from south Pembrokeshire to the Gower Peninsula. Long, sandy beaches and wide, silty estuaries dominate much of the bay, though there are also high cliffs and rocky coves in places.

The Gower Peninsula, at the eastern end of the bay, is a small but priceless gem. Britain's first official Area of Outstanding Natural Beauty (AONB), the peninsula contains an astonishing variety of landscapes: dunes, marshland, high cliffs, windswept downs, wooded valleys, picturesque villages and glorious sandy beaches — all linked by a superb footpath network.

"I have been taught the script of the stones, and I know the tongue of the wave."

Vernon Watkins (1906–67), from *New Selected Poems* (2006)

TOP 10 Walks: Carmarthen Bay & Gower

CARMARTHEN BAY AND THE GOWER PENINSULA offer some of the finest coastal walking in South Wales, rivalling even the Pembrokeshire National Park for beauty and natural variety. Each circular walk has been carefully chosen to highlight what makes this superb stretch of coast so special. You will visit long sandy beaches and historic castles, cross rugged cliffs and windswept downs, and even follow in the footsteps of one of Wales' most famous poets. It's unmissable.

Pendine & Marros — page 8

Laugharne — page 14

Llansteffan — page 20

Pembrey — page 26

Pendine Sands stretches for more than 10 kilometres along the Carmarthenshire coast

Pendine & Marros

A strenuous walk exploring the rugged coastline between Pendine and Marros

What to expect:
Undulating coast path, then fields, woodland and gravel tracks

Distance/time: 10.5km/ 6½ miles. Allow 4 hours

Start: Large Pay and Display car park in Pendine

Grid ref: SN 235 080

Ordnance Survey Map: Explorer 177 Carmarthen & Kidwelly, *Pendine & Laugharne*

After the walk: Cafés and pub in Pendine, as well as the 'Green Bridge Inn' on the walk itself

Walk outline

This tough but rewarding walk traces the wild, rugged coastline between Pendine and Marros. There are some demanding ups and downs, but also stunning views of Pendine Sands and along the coast to Pembrokeshire. The easier return route follows a gravel track inland to Marros and then descends along a wooded valley to the small bay of Morfa Bychan. At low tide, a walk along the beach avoids a strenuous climb and descent over Gilman Point.

Pendine

Historically, Pendine was divided between the old hill-top settlement around the parish church and a harbour settlement. The coastal part of the village grew significantly after the 18th century, when Pendine became a popular seaside resort. During the 1920s, the 10 kilometres of hard, flat sands brought lasting fame for land speed record attempts. Visitors can learn more about its heroic but sometimes tragic history in the Museum of Speed.

The high coastal cliffs to the west of Pendine are unique in Carmarthenshire. They offer extensive panoramic views as well as superb habitat for sea birds and wild flowers.

Shadows on the sands

Fulmar

The Walk

1. From the car park in **Pendine**, walk towards the sea and turn right along the walkway above the beach. Briefly join the main road and then bear left along a line of beach cafés.

At the end of the walkway, follow a **Wales Coast Path** waymark up a steep flight of steps. Climb steeply to the top of the cliffs, enjoying fine views along **Pendine Sands**. Continue over **Gilman Point** — note the Iron Age earthworks at the top — and descend steeply to the small bay of **Morfa Bychan** (not named on the OS map).

2. Cross a track to continue along the coast path. After passing a battered slab of concrete, the path climbs steeply out of the bay along a winding trail.

The concrete slab was part of a Second World War training exercise called 'Exercise Jantzen' in which troops practised storming Morfa Bychan from the sea in preparation for the Normandy landings.

At a junction with a gravel track, follow the waymark left and continue climbing. A short distance ahead, reach a waymark post at the top of the climb (there is a

07

Hidden bay: *The tiny unmarked bay of Morfa Bychan, backed by Gilman Point*

wooden gate ahead). Follow the sign left, downhill towards the sea, and go through a kissing gate. Continue down the slope towards **Ragwen Point**.

In the gorse to the left of the path are several ruined Neolithic burial chambers.

The obvious path soon bears right, cutting across the slope towards **Marros Sands** (parts of the path are much eroded and may be muddy: a boardwalk carries you safely across a particularly boggy section of ground). Ignore a path forking left and continue ahead along the **Wales Coast Path**.

3. The path now follows a more level route, with a fence to the right and Marros Sands below on the left. After a field gate, views are obscured as you enter an area of scrubby woodland. Cross a private track running down to **Marros Sands** and then a stream by a wooden stile and gate. The path climbs right then levels off once more, eventually emerging from the trees onto the access track to **Marros Mill**.

Flat out?: *Pendine's hard, open sands were once popular for land speed record attempts*

Bear right up the hill, turning sharply to the right then left. At the next right-hand bend, leave the Wales Coast Path by continuing uphill along the main track. Follow the track ahead for around 1 kilometre or so until you reach the **church in Marros**.

4. Cross the minor road in Marros to continue along a track opposite the church. Stay with the main track as it bears right and descends to a house in a valley.

Go through the gate ahead marked '**Pwll Cottage**'. Pass in front of the house then bear right across the bottom of the garden towards a gate. Continue alongside a fence through woodland to a field.

Bear slightly right in the field to cross to an obvious gate on the far side. Keep ahead in the next field and then drop slightly left to a gate into a third field. Follow the bridleway (now waymarked) along the bottom of the valley to a set of double gates leading into woodland. Continue ahead to a junction of gravel tracks, then ahead again, up the hill. Pass a metal barn and descend to a junction with a minor road.

5. Turn left down the road. In a dip at the bottom of the hill, turn right down a track marked with a footpath sign (or continue ahead for the **Green Bridge Inn**). The track descends along a narrow wooded valley to the coast at **Morfa Bychan**. If the tide is out, you can return to Pendine along the beach (much easier). Otherwise, you will need to retrace your steps back over **Gilman Point** to complete the walk. ♦

St Lawrence's Church, Marros

With its sturdy defensive tower, Marros Church is typical of those established in Norman 'Englishries' during the 13th and 14th centuries. As well as providing a place of refuge during attacks by Welsh forces, the tower would have served as a useful landmark for ships in Carmarthen Bay. The unusual war memorial on the green outside was inspired by the Neolithic burial chambers above Ragwen Point.

Dylan Thomas' Boathouse at Laugharne

Laugharne

A moderately easy walk exploring the woods and fields around Laugharne

Distance/time: 9.5km/ 6 miles (can be split into two loops). Allow 3½ hours

Start: Free car park in the centre of Laugharne below the castle

Grid ref: SN 301 106

Ordnance Survey Map: Explorer 177 Carmarthen & Kidwelly, *Pendine & Laugharne*

After the walk: Cafés, pubs and restaurants in Laugharne, and a tearoom near the end of the walk in Dylan Thomas' Boathouse

Walk outline

From Laugharne a good-quality path climbs steeply across wooded slopes with fine estuary views before descending to an easy level track below Sir John's Hill. Roads and field paths lead back towards Laugharne, allowing the route to be shortened. The full walk continues past the parish church, rejoining the coast path north of Laugharne. The walk returns through fields and woodland alongside the River Taf, passing Dylan Thomas' Boathouse on the edge of town.

Laugharne

Quirky little Laugharne is famous for its association with Dylan Thomas. Dylan regarded the town as his spiritual home and spent the final four years of his life here. The town features in a number of well-known poems, notably 'Poem in October' and 'Over Sir John's Hill', and also helped to inspire Dylan's last major work, 'Under Milk Wood'.

But there is more to Laugharne than Dylan Thomas. Particularly impressive are the views across the Taf Estuary from the slopes above the town. The estuary is an important habitat for ducks, geese and waders, and a fascinating landscape in its own right.

Dylan Thomas' writing room

Curlew

The Walk

1. From the car park in **Laugharne**, walk south, away from the castle, with the marshland on your left. At the end of the parking area, pass through a barrier onto a lane signposted as 'Dylan's Birthday Walk' and continue towards a pumping station. At another sign just before the station, bear right uphill onto a woodland trail.

This section of path is known locally as the 'New Walk' and was constructed by Laugharne's town corporation in 1856 to provide access to cockle beds on the marshes. The path now forms part of a short walk from Laugharne tracing the inspiration behind 'Poem in October'.

At the top of the hill there is a brief level section before you reach an information board and **viewpoint** by a path fork. Take the left-hand path, signed 'To The Last Verse', and descend steeply.

At the bottom of the hill, cross a stile onto a track and keep ahead. Continue around the base of **Sir John's Hill** to **Salt House Farm**, which is bypassed via a track on the left. Once past the farm, keep ahead along the access

track to a T-junction with a minor road opposite **Coygen Quarry**.

2. Turn right and climb steeply. As the gradient lessens, bear right onto a dead-end lane. Continue through concrete bollards at the end of the road and keep ahead along the A4066 (no pavement).

After about 400 metres, turn left onto the lane to **Llansadurnen**. Almost immediately, cross a lay-by on the right and aim for a stile. Continue ahead along the right-hand edge of a field.

Sentinel on the Taf: *Laugharne Castle sits on a low bluff overlooking the Taf estuary*

Looking up the slope to the left, it is possible to make out the remains of medieval strip fields. These were granted to burgesses of the town by Laugharne Corporation and are separated by lines of unploughed grass.

Do not cross the metal stile ahead, but bear left to a field boundary corner and continue with the hedge on your right. Join an enclosed sunken path and descend to a house. Keep ahead behind the house and join the access track downhill. This becomes a narrow lane running alongside a stream.

3. At a T-junction with a wider road, turn right and descend towards **Laugharne**. Immediately after passing 30mph signs, take a road on the left (or continue ahead to return to the centre of town). On a sharp right-hand bend, bear left into **Holloway Road**, a narrow, dead-end passage between houses.

Continue onto an enclosed path and then ahead along a well-worn path across fields. At the end of the second field, turn right onto a minor road and

Watery panorama: *The broad Taf estuary at low tide, seen from Laugharne Castle*

arrive at a T-junction with the A4066. Turn right, then left through the lych gate of **St Martin's Church**.

This 13th-century church lies some distance from Laugharne, built on the site of an earlier Celtic church predating the existence of the town. Dylan Thomas's grave is in the new cemetery across the footbridge and is marked by a white cross.

Climb to the church and follow the path around the back of the building to the left. Keep ahead onto a grassy path and pass through a kissing gate to a lane.

Turn left and climb steadily for around 500 metres. Just after a left-hand bend, reach a T-junction and turn right. The lane immediately turns to a gravel track and shortly forks. Keep ahead down the steep track to Delacorse. You are now back on the **Wales Coast Path**.

4. At the bottom of the hill, follow the track past **Delacorse** to a kissing gate. Continue along the bottom edge of fields with the **River Taf** to your left. After about 500 metres, the path leaves the fields to join a woodland trail above the estuary.

Soon after crossing a private road, you join a narrow lane above **Dylan**

Thomas' Boathouse. Ignore any steps descending on the left and continue along the lane to a T-junction. Turn left downhill then bear left again where the road bends to the right.

Pass **Seaview** and turn left in front of **Coach House** towards **Castle Cottage**. A narrow passage leads off to the right and drops to a wide path below **Laugharne Castle**. Bear right to return to your starting point. ◆

Laugharne Castle

Although founded by the Normans, most of the existing castle is the work of Sir John Perrot, who converted the medieval building into a substantial Tudor mansion. Badly damaged in the Civil War, this was left to decay and later incorporated into the grounds of Castle House. In the 1930s, the gazebo overlooking the estuary was used as a writing room by both Richard Hughes and Dylan Thomas.

Llansteffan Castle is perched high above the Towy Estuary

Llansteffan

A varied double loop with fantastic views across Carmarthen Bay and the county's 'three rivers'

What to expect:
Beach, coast path, farm tracks and fields; shorter walk possible

Distance/time: 7km/ 4¼ miles (can be shortened further if required). Allow 3 hours

Start: Free car park at the south end of Llansteffan's beach

Grid ref: SN 352 104

Ordnance Survey Map: Explorer 177 Carmarthen & Kidwelly, *Pendine & Laugharne*

After the walk: Cafés, pubs and restaurants in Llansteffan; Llansteffan Castle is a must see and makes a great picnic spot

Walk outline

At low tide, the beach provides a pleasant alternative to the coast path between Llansteffan and Scott's Bay. A steadily ascending path leads up to Wharley Point and spectacular views. The route now heads back to Scott's Bay, joining a descending field track from Lord's Park. The walk can be shortened by retracing your outward route, but missing the fantastic views from the fields above Llansteffan.

Llansteffan

Llansteffan is noted for its Georgian architecture and tranquil estuary. The dignified houses reflect the village's popularity as a wealthy resort in the 18th and early 19th centuries. After 1852, the arrival of the railway in neighbouring Ferryside also allowed miners from the South Wales valleys to holiday in the village. A ferry transported visitors across the Towy from the station to 'The Green'.

Llansteffan Castle keep

Llansteffan's Norman castle perches spectacularly on a craggy promontory above the River Towy. The castle is sited on the remains of an earlier Iron Age fort and provides extensive panoramic views across Carmarthen Bay and the surrounding countryside.

Sea lavender

Carmarthen Bay. There is no better place to appreciate the full extent of the bay, which stretches from Caldey Island near Tenby to Worms Head on the Gower Peninsula. At low tide, extensive areas of sand are uncovered. Silting in the bay became an increasing problem during the 19th century and contributed to a decline in the prosperity of local ports.

The Walk

1. From the car park in **Llansteffan**, head for the beach and turn right. If the tide allows, follow the beach round to **Scott's Bay** and join the coast path in front of **St Anthony's Cottage**. Otherwise, leave the beach along a narrow lane and fork immediately left up steps. Join the **Wales Coast Path** and continue over the wooded cliff top to **Scott's Bay**.

From Scott's Bay, climb steadily across steep wooded slopes to **Wharley Point**.

This splendid viewpoint overlooks the confluence of the Taf, Towy and Gwendraeth rivers as they merge in the shallow, shimmering waters of

2. Once round the headland, the path bears right, away from the sea, and drops to a lane. Turn right along the road, following a sign for 'Llanstephan Castle'. Continue along the track to the left of **Lord's Park** (the path is well signed past the farm) and join a grassy track along the right-hand edge of fields.

Your route descends to the right of a steep-sided valley, eventually leaving the fields to join an enclosed path back to the coast path at **Scott's Bay**. Turn left and retrace your steps in front of St Anthony's Cottage. Immediately after crossing the stone bridge over the stream, take a waymarked path on the left.

Out to sea: *A walker contemplates the view from the Wales Coast Path at Wharley Point*

At this point, you can shorten the walk — and avoid a steep climb through fields — by returning to Llansteffan along the coast path or beach.

3. The path runs alongside a wall bordering St Anthony's Cottage.

Look out for a door on the left marked 'Ffynnon Antwn Sant' ('St Anthony's Well'). Although it appears private, you may go through to view the well (further details below).

Join the access track from St Anthony's Cottage and climb gently to a gate. Go through and turn immediately left into **Parc-Glâs**, crossing in front of the house to a stile into a field. Turn right in the field and climb steeply along its right-hand boundary. At the top, cross a stile on the right and follow the hedge to the left. Continue along the left-hand boundary of a third field, curving slightly left to meet a road.

This quiet country lane was one of the major highways of medieval Wales. Known

Castle view: *Llansteffan Castle overlooks the broad sands of the Towy Estuary*

as 'The King's Way', it connected south and west Wales via two ferry crossings on the rivers Taf and Towy. The road remained an important highway until the 18th century, when the development of turnpikes led to quicker, more direct routes across Wales.

4. Cross the road to a stile and follow the left-hand edge of a field ahead. Bear slightly left across a second field to a stile onto a lane. Turn left and then immediately right, along the access track to Lanfach.

At a fork near the farm, keep ahead onto a grassy path alongside the hedge on your right. This shortly reaches a gate and stile leading into a field. Follow the right-hand edge of three fields downhill towards Llansteffan. At the bottom of the third field, cross a stile to the right of a stone wall onto an enclosed path. Continue downhill to emerge in the centre of **Llansteffan** between the Castle Inn and the Sticks Hotel.

Cross the main street to continue along **Church Road** opposite. To the right is the 'Old Pound' (now a shop) and the parish church. At the end of the houses,

turn left onto a tarmac path (part of the **Wales Coast Path**) to return to your starting point above the beach.

Before returning to your vehicle, it is recommended that you continue along Church Road to its end and climb the private drive up to **Llansteffan Castle**. Entry is free and rewarded with panoramic views from the top. ♦

St Anthony's Well

The original St Anthony (c.251–c.356) was an early Christian hermit from Egypt whose ascetic example helped to spread the concept of monasticism. In the 6th century, a local Welsh hermit, Antwn (Anthony), took the name of his Egyptian predecessor and used the well to baptise Christian converts. The well's waters were later reputed to have healing powers and attracted pilgrims travelling the King's Way to St David's.

Looking towards the Gower from the dunes at Pembrey Burrows

Pembrey

A lovely little walk exploring the hills and levels around the village of Pembrey

What to expect:
Woodland paths, tracks and minor roads; possible mud near farm

Distance/time: 7km/ 4½ miles. Allow 3 hours

Start: Forestry Commission car park at Penybedd Wood

Grid ref: SN 419 013

Ordnance Survey Map: Explorer 164 Gower, *Llanelli*

After the walk: Pubs in Pembrey; picnic site at Penybedd Wood

Walk outline

A waymarked forestry trail leads through Penybedd Wood. A track and minor road take the route on to Ffrwd Farm Mire Nature Reserve and a level path along the line of the former Ashburnham Canal. After a meandering ascent across steep wooded slopes, the route enters farmland near Penllwyn Isaf. There are great views of the Gower Peninsula, then a steep descent into Pembrey. Roads lead back to the car park at Penybedd Wood.

Pembrey

Some 6,000 years ago, the sea would have lapped the foot of the high ground behind Pembrey. Natural deposition was later accelerated by building sea walls and draining the land. This process of land reclamation, begun in the late Middle Ages, was not fully completed until the start of the 19th century. In the 1930s, Pembrey Forest was planted to stabilise the dunes behind Cefn Sidan Sands.

The village retained access to the sea, briefly flourishing as an industrial port in the early 19th century. The remains of former railways and canals still criss-cross the area, providing pathways rich with historic interest.

Saltmarsh ponies

Sedge warbler

Sea of reeds: *A raised boardwalk winds into the reeds at Ffrwd Farm Mire Nature Reserve*

The Walk

1. Facing **Penybedd Wood** from the car park, take the waymarked path on the right. This grassy trail meanders through mostly open woodland, then curves left to meet a gravel forestry track. Turn right and continue to a wooden gate at the far end of the forest.

The path from the car park can sometimes be waterlogged after heavy rain. If this is the case, follow the main gravel track.

Go through the gate and continue along the track to the left of **Forest House**. Follow this pot-holed track across flat, marshy grazing to **Penybedd**. With farm buildings to the left, turn right towards a level crossing. A short distance beyond is the **A484**.

2. Cross to a lane opposite and continue ahead. As the lane curves left, take a signed footpath on the right into **Ffrwd Farm Mire Nature Reserve**. This passes through a kissing gate and continues along a grassy embankment between trees.

The path through the reserve follows the line of the former Asburnham Canal. This was funded by Lord Ashburnham to transport coal from his pits in Coed Rhyal to ships on the Gwendraeth Estuary. By 1818, the coal had been exhausted and the canal was subsequently abandoned.

Ffrwd Fen (Ffrwd Farm Mire) is a nature reserve that is owned and managed by the Wildlife Trust of South and West Wales. An information board to the side of the path explains the reserve's importance to wildlife, while a boardwalk leads out to a viewing area overlooking the marsh.

At the end of the reserve, cross a two-way road and continue up a track opposite. As the track starts curving left to a house, follow the 'Mountain Walks' sign up a grassy slope to the right. Enter woodland and take the path to the left, along the bottom edge of the trees; it's signposted 'St Illtyd's Walk'.

At a junction of paths above the house, turn left to continue along the bottom edge of the wood. The path is rugged

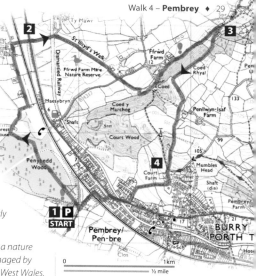

and undulating, but soon drops to a lane above **Ffrwd Farm**. Turn right and climb steadily, enjoying fine views toward Kidwelly and Llansaint.

3. After about 600 metres, turn sharply right onto a track and go through a gate marked 'Cwm yr Erfin'. Where signs indicate private property ahead, bear right onto a waymarked grassy path above a fence. Enter woodland and shortly follow the path left, up a steeply stepped section. At the top of the steps, turn right and climb gently until you emerge from the trees.

The tide is high: *Semi-wild ponies graze the open dunes and saltmarshes at Pembrey*

Leave **Coed Rhyal** by a stile and continue between thick scrub along the left-hand edge of a field (after wet weather, this section of path can be badly churned up by livestock). Where the scrub opens out, ignore the track ahead to **Penllwyn Isaf** and instead turn right, cutting straight across the field to a stile on the far side.

In the next field, bear slightly left to a stile in the far corner, then continue along the right-hand edge of two fields, shortly enjoying fabulous views over the Gower Peninsula and Loughor

Estuary. Descend steeply to a kissing gate (just to the left of a large, red-brick house) and continue downhill along an enclosed path. Join a road descending into **Pembrey** and shortly turn right onto a tarmac path below the ruins of **Court Farm**.

The history of Court Farm dates back to medieval times, when Pembrey was a manor within the Norman lordship of Kidwelly. (The footpath below the building is equally old — a medieval route to Penybedd.) The house was rebuilt in the Elizabethan period and later came into the possession of the Ashburnham family of Sussex. Now an overgrown ruin, it remains

structurally sound, raising hopes that it may one day be restored.

4. Join a residential road at the end of the path, soon meeting a T-junction with the A484 in **Pembrey**. Follow the pavement right, crossing the road at a traffic island a short distance ahead. Take the next road on the left, signed 'Country Park', and follow it back to the car park at **Penybedd Wood**. ♦

St Illtyd

Among Welsh saints, St Illtyd is second in importance only to St David. His most famous act occurred in Llantwit Major, where he founded a monastery in AD 508 that served as a divinity school for early Christians. A number of Welsh churches are dedicated to Illtyd, including the sizable parish church in Pembrey. More recently, a long-distance trail between Pembrey and Margam has also been named after the saint.

The dunes, forest and Cwm Ivy Tor at Whiteford Nature Reserve

Whiteford

An easy level walk around the dunes and marshes of Whiteford

What to expect:
Woods, sea wall, dunes, conifers and long sandy beach

Distance/time: 8km/ 5 miles. Allow 3 hours

Start: Whitford Beach Car Park at the western end of Llanmadoc village (£1 honesty box)

Grid ref: SS 439 934

Ordnance Survey Map: Explorer 164 Gower, *Llanelli*

After the walk: The Britannia Inn in Llanmadoc is a short drive from the start

Walk outline

The route follows a path along the bottom edge of Cwm Ivy Woods, then along the top of a sea wall across Cwm Ivy Marsh. A track runs north between Whiteford Burrows and the marshes, then continues as a path through stands of tall pine trees to Whiteford Point. The return leg is along the long, sandy beach of Whiteford Sands to Cwm Ivy Tor. A track and lane complete the round.

Whiteford

This low-lying peninsula of mud, sand and marshland is one of the most remote and peaceful spots in Gower. It is hard to believe that this tranquil nature reserve has seen quarrying, sand extraction, land reclamation and even service as an army firing range — all within the fairly recent past.

Cwm Ivy National Trust sign

Sandwiched between sea and estuary, Whiteford is characterised by a tremendous variety of habitat: dunes, beach, salt marsh, mud flats and woodland can all be found within its 3,000 acres. Wildfowl and waders winter along the Loughor Estuary, while in the spring butterflies and blossoming wild flowers transform the dunes into a blaze of vibrant colour.

Silver washed fritillary

The Walk

1. Turn right out of the car park and descend along the lane towards **Cwm Ivy**. Fork right in front of the houses and then right again, down a rough track signed as a footpath.

Continue onto a path along the bottom edge of **Cwm Ivy Woods**. At a junction with the **Wales Coast Path**, turn left through the gate. Cross **Cwm Ivy Marsh** along the top of the sea wall.

The wall dates from the 17th century and was built to reclaim a section of Cwm Ivy Marsh from the sea. East of the wall, a vast salt marsh extends the entire length of the north Gower coast.

2. At the end of the wall, turn right, towards 'Whiteford', and follow a track along the boundary between burrows and salt marsh. As the track curves left, away from the marsh, bear slightly right onto a narrower path. This is marked as part of the **Wales Coast Path** and continues to follow the marshland edge. (If the official path is flooded, it is possible to carry on along the track, meeting up with the coast path later.)

Where directed, bear slightly left, away from the marsh, and pass through conifers planted to stabilise

the dunes. The path is well marked and emerges at an information board on the edge of a sandy beach facing the **Loughor Estuary**. Keep ahead to a waymark post in the sand and follow the arrow left along the beach towards **Whiteford Point**.

At low tide, it is possible to walk across the sand and rock to Whiteford Point Lighthouse. If you do, beware of rapid incoming tides that can quickly surround you.

3. Follow the beach around the headland and then along the length of **Whiteford Sands**. Where the

0   1km
                    1 mile

Away from it all: *A lone walker enjoys a moment of solitude near Whiteford Point*

high tide line begins to curve right, leave the beach and join a waymarked track in the direction of Cwm Ivy Tor. Follow a fence to a corner and then turn sharply left to reach a gate and junction to the right of conifers.

Take the left-hand track, signposted to 'Cwm Ivy', and pass directly below the steep grassy slope of **Cwm Ivy Tor**. Ignore the track on the left and keep straight ahead up the hill. Go through a gate onto a lane in **Cwm Ivy** and retrace your outward route up the hill to **Whitford Beach Car Park**. ♦

Whiteford Point Lighthouse
During the 19th century, the rapid growth of Llanelli and Burry Port turned the shallow waters of the Loughor Estuary into a busy shipping channel. Built to a unique cast-iron design, Whiteford Point Lighthouse was constructed by the Llanelli harbour authorities around 1865 to mark a particularly dangerous shoal off Whiteford Point. Following Llanelli's decline as a port, the light was finally extinguished in the 1920s.

A sun-warmed tidal pool at Broughton Bay, near Llangennith

Llangennith

A moderately easy walk exploring the beautiful coastal scenery west of Llangennith

What to expect:
Lanes, tracks, coast path and beach; generally good-quality paths

Distance/time: 8.25km/ 5¼ miles. Allow 3 hours

Start: Park considerately near the church in Llangennith; if required, there is alternative parking further round the route at Hillend Camping & Caravan Park

Grid ref: SS 428 914

Ordnance Survey Map: Explorer 164 Gower, *Llanelli*

After the walk: Excellent pub in Llangennith, as well as café at Hillend Camping & Caravan Park

Walk outline

A lane, track and field path take the route from Llangennith to the coast at Broughton Bay. From here, a lovely section of coast path climbs through dunes to a grassy cliff top before dropping to Rhossili Bay. A glorious beach walk follows as far as Hillend, where the route turns inland through a campsite and joins a grassy bridleway around the base of Rhossili Down. A rough track and lane lead back to Llangennith.

Llangennith

In the mid-19th century, Llangennith was a thriving community with eight working mills and a large population engaged in rural industries. It was also a village with an unparalleled reputation for drunkenness and lawlessness. Historic festivals and traditions were often a pretext for drunken, riotous behaviour, with the feast of St Cenydd on 5th July being a notorious day for 'merrymaking'.

St Cenydd himself was a 6th-century saint around whom a number of colourful legends developed. The lych gate of the parish church depicts Cenydd as an unwanted child cast adrift on the River Loughor, being fed by gulls.

Llangennith dunes

Stonechat

Island in the tide: *The tiny island of Burry Holms is cut off by the tide twice a day*

The Walk

1. Facing the **King's Head**, turn left down **Llangennith's main street**. Turn right in front of 20mph signs onto a track along the left-hand wall of a house. Bear left and continue along a short section of path to a road.

Turn right and follow the lane as it bears left and climbs out of the village. Continue along the base of **Llanmadoc Hill**, then descend gently between hedges. Where the lane ends, continue along an enclosed track, signposted to 'Broughton Beach', to the left of Ty'r Ceiliog.

After a gate, the track descends across an open field towards Broughton Bay. At a right-hand bend, keep ahead through two kissing gates and continue down the right-hand side of two fields towards the sea. Reach a junction with the **Wales Coast Path** and turn left, signed to 'Rhossili'.

2. Join a track past **Broughton Farm**. At the end of the buildings, bear right onto a grassy track to the right of static caravans. Bear slightly left onto a road through the caravan park and follow it round to the left. As the road straightens, turn sharp right at a waymark post onto a short dead-end road between caravans. An obvious path continues ahead along the coast.

Follow **Wales Coast Path** waymarks along the boardwalk up the hill (a detour along a footpath to the right will take you to a viewpoint above **Twlc Point**). At the top, join a grassy path

through the burrows to the cliffs above **Bluepool Corner**, where a sandy beach is visible at low tide.

This small bay is accessible only by foot at low tide and involves a scramble at the bottom. The blue pool from which the bay gets its name is a circular rock pool some 15 feet in diameter and 8 feet deep. Because of its consistent depth and surrounding high rocks, the pool is a popular diving spot.

Continue along the cliffs and shortly descend a grassy slope towards the tidal

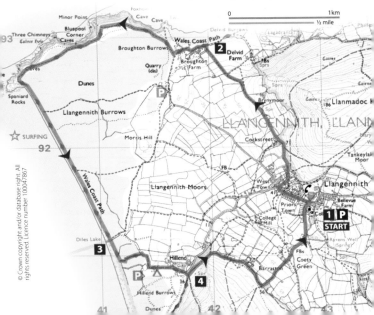

Sun and sea: *Emerging from the dunes at Llangennith onto the sands of Rhossili Bay*

island of **Burry Holms**. Do not descend onto the stony causeway, but bear left along a grassy path until it becomes possible to drop onto the long, sandy beach of **Rhossili Bay**.

The three-mile stretch of sand between Burry Holms and Worms Head is one of the most spectacular beaches in Britain. Backed by dunes in the north and Rhossili Down in the south, the beach is naturally protected from any form of commercial development and endowed with a powerful sense of wild splendour.

3. Follow the beach south as far as **Diles Lake**, a small stream draining Llangennith Moors. Pass the stream and in 200 metres, turn left onto a waymarked path through the dunes.

Turn right at a track, shortly reaching a car park. Follow the track left, up the hill, and keep ahead through Hillend Camping & Caravan Park to the main entrance. Turn right immediately after the entrance through a gate onto **Rhossili Down**.

4. Take the path to the left, which climbs steadily, roughly parallel to the road below. Ignore a smaller path bearing left down the hill, instead staying with the

main path as it curves right and joins the bottom edge of the common.

Continue past two houses, then join an obvious track down the common edge to the left. Keep ahead through a gate and descend along an enclosed track to **Coety Green**, where traces of old cottages and a corn mill can be seen. Follow the lane up the hill to return to the centre of **Llangennith**. ♦

Burry Holms

Burry Holms is a tidal island, accessible for a few hours either side of low tide. There are traces of a small medieval hermitage dedicated to St Cenydd on the island, as well as a defensive ditch from the earlier Iron Age. A few centuries after St Cenydd's occupation, the island was possibly used as a base by Viking raiders. Llangennith itself was sacked and pillaged in 986.

Worms Head and Rhossili Bay from the top of Rhossili Down

Rhossili

A stunning but sometimes demanding walk savouring the iconic coastal scenery of Rhossili

What to expect:
Steep climb then good tracks and coast path; avoidable exposed section

Distance/time: 7.25km/ 4½ miles. Allow 3 hours

Start: Large National Trust car park at the western end of Rhossili (fee payable)

Grid ref: SS 416 880

Ordnance Survey Map: Explorer 164 Gower, *Llanelli*

After the walk: Cafés and pub in Rhossili

Walk outline

This fabulous walk begins with a steep pull to the top of Rhossili Down. The reward is a fabulous panoramic view from the highest point on the peninsula. The route then bears south-east, leaving the down and dropping to the coast at Mewslade Bay. An exposed path (avoidable if required) carves across the cliffs to join the Wales Coast Path. Grassy cliff-tops lead to Worms Head and the track back to Rhossili.

Rhossili

Although the name Rhossili is Welsh in origin, the village became part of English-speaking Gower following the Norman conquest of the peninsula in the 12th century and was settled extensively from the west of England. In the troubled centuries that followed, it remained vulnerable to raids from hostile Welsh neighbours. As a result, the village church was provided with a strong tower that could act as a place of refuge during times of warfare and raiding.

Path above Mewslade Bay

Those days are long gone and the village is better known today for its stunning natural scenery and iconic coastal views. The long sandy beach is regularly voted among the best in Europe.

Atlantic grey seal

The Walk

1. Turn right out of the car park in **Rhossili** and follow the road back up through the village. Bear left through the bus turning area to a path behind the church. Turn left at a track and keep ahead to a gate onto **Rhossili Down**. Go through and climb steeply to the trig point on the summit of the **Beacon**.

At 193 metres above sea level, the Beacon is the highest point on the Gower Peninsula and commands sweeping views over the Bristol Channel, Carmarthen Bay and east towards Swansea. On a clear day it is possible to see the Brecon Beacons, as well as Pembrokeshire and Devon.

2. From the 'trig' point, retrace your steps for a few metres, then bear left, onto

a wide grassy path heading roughly south-east. Continue down the widest, most obvious path, eventually joining a gravel track by a covered reservoir. Descend between banks to a junction with a lane opposite **Talgarth Well**.

Cross to a stile to the left of the drive opposite and follow a diverted footpath around the perimeter of the property. Continue down an enclosed path to a track and turn right down the hill. Join a lane and shortly reach a junction with the B4247 in **Pitton**.

Bear right across the main road to continue along a lane to the right of **Corner Farm House**. Just past a car

0   1km
       ½ mile

Best beach?: *Rhossili's beautiful beach is regularly voted the best in Wales*

park, follow a sign for 'Mewslade Bay' to the right and pass between barns onto a path through woodland. Emerging from the trees, take the left, lower fork to continue down the valley towards Mewslade Bay.

The narrow, exposed path around the back of **Mewslade Bay** is not to everyone's taste and is certainly not suitable for young children. To avoid this potentially dangerous section of the route, take the right, upper fork when

you emerge from the trees and shortly join the **Wales Coast Path** along the boundary of the coastal common.

3. Keep straight across the Wales Coast Path, still descending between limestone cliffs. Just before **Mewslade Bay**, bear right onto a narrow trail and climb gently across the cliffs. At a stepped, rocky area, make sure you join the higher ledge to the right and follow the narrow, briefly exposed path as it curves around the corner of the headland. Staying well away from the crumbling cliff edge, bear left across a

A long way out: *The amazing Worm's Head promontory juts a mile out into the sea*

grassy area and follow the path ahead towards the corner of a dry-stone wall.

Rejoin the Wales Coast Path and continue ahead along a grassy cliff-top path. This runs close to the boundary wall until a stony section of path descends through a limestone bluff above **Fall Bay**. Do not descend to the beach, but bear slightly left to continue on the waymarked upper path above the bay.

4. Your target is a dry-stone wall at the western end of Fall Bay. Join the wall and then follow it up the headland to the right. Continue across the grassy cliff top, keeping ahead towards a coastguard lookout station where the waymarked coast path follows the wall to the right.

This old coastguard lookout station is now an information point manned by volunteers. A sign outside publicises the safe crossing times to Worms Head each day.

From the **coastguard building**, turn right along a wide grassy strip and join the gravel track leading back to **Rhossili**.

As you approach the village, there are

stunning views along the full length of Rhossili Bay. Study the sand carefully at low tide and you will also be able to make out the remains of a ship, the Helvetia, which foundered in November 1887. Before modern navigational equipment, the jagged rocks of Worms Head made the coast near Rhossili particularly dangerous to shipping: over thirty wrecks have been identified in Rhossili Bay, most from the late 19th and early 20th centuries. ◆

Worms Head

The narrow tidal promontory of Worms Head is one of Gower's most iconic natural attractions. Its name derives from the Old English word for dragon and relates to the headland's distinctive outline: three high sections linked by a long, slender neck. Now a nature reserve, the headland is joined to the mainland via a rocky causeway for only 2½ hours either side of low tide.

Looking up the coast from Oxwich towards Great Tor headland

Oxwich

A mainly coastal walk exploring the cliffs and woods of Oxwich Point

What to expect:
Lane, woods, fields and coast path, steep climb and descent to finish

Distance/time: 7.25km/ 4½ miles. Allow 3 hours

Start: Large beach-side car park in Oxwich (fee payable)

Grid ref: SS 502 864

Ordnance Survey Map: Explorer 164 Gower, *Llanelli*

After the walk: Pub and beach café in Oxwich

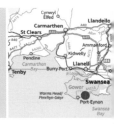

Walk outline

The walk initially heads away from the sea, climbing inland along a lane to Oxwich Green. A path via Oxwich Castle adds interest to this section. From Oxwich Green, the route crosses fields then drops through coastal scrub to Slade Bay or 'The Sands'. The rest of the walk hugs the coast closely, following the shore back around Oxwich Point to Oxwich. A steep climb and descent through Oxwich Wood concludes the round.

Oxwich

A cluster of motte-and-bailey castles around Oxwich Bay suggests that the area acted as a beachhead for the Norman invasion of the peninsula in the 12th century. Some 400 years later, the castle at Oxwich was rebuilt by the Mansel family as a grand Tudor manor house.

Like many parts of the south Gower coast, Oxwich Point was at one time the site of extensive limestone quarrying. The headland's steep northern slopes are now clothed in deciduous trees, concealing the scars of past industry. This broadleaf woodland forms part of Oxwich National Nature Reserve and is filled in spring with the heady scent of wild garlic.

Oxwich Castle

Bee orchid

The Walk

1. From the car park, head towards the beach and turn right. Go through a gap in a wall opposite the **Oxwich Bay Hotel** and turn right along the lane back to **Oxwich**. At a crossroads in the village, turn left onto a dead-end lane signed to 'Slade and Oxwich Castle'.

Ignore a path on the left signed to 'Oxwich Point', continuing instead to a second path with the same sign. Climb through woodland to **Oxwich Castle** and bear right between farm buildings. Follow the track sharp right in front of the castle and bear left across a field.

Cross an old stone stile in the far corner of the field and rejoin the lane. Turn left and follow the road through **Oxwich Green**, ignoring another sign for 'Oxwich Point' by a telephone box and bus stop. About 100 metres farther on, take the next footpath on the left, signed to 'Slade Bay and Horton'.

2. The path forks right along a concrete track and then continues along a grassy track above static caravans. Cross a stile and follow a well-marked path through fields, initially to the left. After leaving the fields, the path descends obliquely to the right through scrub. At a level section not far from the sea, take a path marked 'Coast Path Diversion' dropping to the coast on the left.

3. Emerge above a tidal beach — 'The Sands' — and follow the **Wales Coast Path** left. Initially, the path is narrow and squeezed between a fence on the left and a low cliff edge, but soon opens out onto a wide grassy area between cliffs and the sea. Continue round **Oxwich Point**, with views opening up along the coast ahead. Pass through a kissing gate into **Oxwich National Nature Reserve** and shortly enter **Oxwich Wood**.

Horsing around: *Semi-wild commoners' ponies below the cliffs near Oxwich Point*

Continue along the lower edge of the wood for around 500 metres before following the path left, up a long, steep hill. At the top, turn right along the upper woodland edge before dropping slightly to a signed fork. Take the right-hand path, marked 'Coast Path' and 'Oxwich Beach', and descend a long flight of steps to the sea. Turn left at the bottom, past **St Illtyd's Church**, and continue along a lane to the **Oxwich Bay Hotel**. Go through a gap in the wall on the right and retrace your steps across the beach to the car park. ♦

Oxwich National Nature Reserve

There are very few coastal areas in Britain that can rival Oxwich Bay's diversity of habitat. Within a relatively small area can be found dunes, beach, woodland, salt marsh and freshwater marsh, all teeming with wildlife. Around 600 species of plant have been recorded along the reserve's wooded cliffs, while the bay's marshy reedbeds are home to a variety of warblers and even the rare European bittern.

A hot summer afternoon at Three Cliffs Bay

Pennard

An exceptionally scenic walk along the high coastal cliffs of Pennard

Distance/time: 9.5km/ 6 miles (can be split into two loops). Allow 3½ hours

Start: National Trust Pay and Display car park in Southgate

Grid ref: SS 553 874

Ordnance Survey Map: Explorer 164 Gower, *Llanelli*

After the walk: Café adjacent to car park

Walk outline
Easy walking along a grassy cliff top leads to Pwlldu Head and stunning views along the Gower coastline. Passing above Pwlldu Bay, the walk descends along a lovely wooded valley into the Bishopston Valley. A direct return to Southgate is possible, but the main route continues across fields and a golf course to Pennard Castle and a splendid view of Three Cliffs Bay. A sandy path and grassy cliff top complete the round.

Pennard
The names Pennard and Southgate are often used interchangeably. The original medieval settlement lay to the north-west, around Pennard Castle, but was abandoned in 1532 due to encroaching sand dunes. The village then found a new centre at St Mary's Church, some 2 kilometres to the east. Suburbanisation in the 20th century led to new settlement around Southgate.

Fortunately, Pennard's stunning coastal cliffs remain unspoilt and offer some of the finest coastal walking on Gower. Keep an eye out for red-billed choughs, a rare, crow-like bird that has recently reappeared on Pennard's cliffs after 100 years' absence.

Three cows at Three Cliffs

Chough

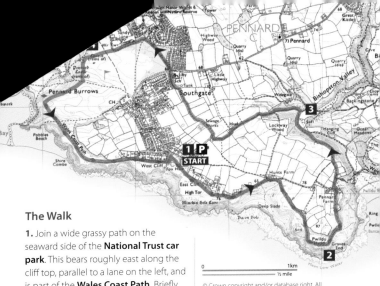

The Walk

1. Join a wide grassy path on the seaward side of the **National Trust car park**. This bears roughly east along the cliff top, parallel to a lane on the left, and is part of the **Wales Coast Path**. Briefly join the lane near **Hunts Farm** and then turn right almost immediately onto a path signed to 'Pwlldu Head'.

Continue along a grassy path across open cliffs. Follow waymarks out to the far end of the headland, enjoying stunning views back along the coast towards Pennard Cliffs.

2. From **Pwlldu Head**, bear left to join a stepped path descending steeply to the north-east. At the bottom of the slope, keep ahead to a waymark post, then follow the arrow steeply uphill to the left. Go through a gate and continue between hedges, the path soon levelling off near a good view of Pwlldu Bay on the right. Keep ahead through

fields and a small copse to reach a junction with a track near **Pennard Farm**.

Bear right at the track, following a sign for 'Pwlldu Bay'. Descend quite sharply to a gate into the grounds of a house. Leave the coast path by bearing left, up a grassy slope, to a stile. Follow the path along the edge of the garden into a field and continue ahead with the field boundary to the right. A grassy path between hedges leads into a second, much larger field. Keep ahead again, following the right-hand boundary along a woodland edge.

Continue for some distance, gradually

Sitting pretty: *The view back along the coast from the cliffs near Pennard*

curving left, until a dip is reached. Cross a stile into the woods and take the path bearing slightly left, downhill past the remains of a stile. This becomes a clear path descending obliquely into the **Bishopston Valley**. Where a path joins from the right, keep ahead, following the sign for 'Kittle and Bishopston', and drop to join the banks of a small river. Where the path and river curve right, take a wide, stony bridleway on the left, following a faded sign for 'Southgate'.

3. Follow the woodland track up the hill and back out of the Bishopston Valley. On leaving the trees, the track levels off and continues between hedges to **Hael Farm**. Keep ahead past the farmhouse, then swing left and right to continue along the farm access track. At a left-hand bend facing a bungalow, turn right and cross a stile into a field.

Alternatively, you can shorten the walk at this point by continuing along the lane into **Southgate**.

Follow the field boundary to the left, then cross a stile onto a path below

Beautiful bay: *A stunning aerial panorama of the beach and cliffs at Three Cliffs Bay*

trees. This continues into a second field, where the field boundary is followed to the right. Keep ahead through two further fields to reach an enclosed path between fences. Fork right at a junction with a gravel path (playing fields to the left) and continue between houses and a school to emerge at a road.

Cross the road to **Linkside Drive** and turn left onto a gravel track marked as a byway. As this curves right, keep ahead onto a waymarked route across the burrows marked with blue bridleway

arrows. The arrows soon run out, but continue roughly parallel to the track until the boundary of the common is approached, then bear left towards a prominent **concrete water tower**. Once past the tower, keep straight ahead across a **golf course** and join a waymarked gravel path running gently downhill towards **Pennard Castle**.

4. Turn left at the castle and follow an intermittent boardwalk along the edge of the high ground overlooking **Pennard Pill**. After about 600 metres, you will rejoin the **Wales Coast Path** as it climbs steeply out of **Three Cliffs Bay**. Continue along the waymarked route,

eventually descending on wooden slats into a shallow, sandy valley to the left of **Pobbles Beach**.

Climb up the far slope of the valley on a steep, sandy path that later turns to grass. Near the top, bear left onto one of the many paths across the grassy cliff top to meet a lane in front of houses. Follow the lane back to the National Trust car park in **Southgate**. ◆

Pennard Castle

This dramatic ruin was probably built in the late 13th century to replace an earlier ringwork defence. Commanding views to the north and west seemed to provide the ideal location for a castle. However, its Norman lords could not have foreseen the problem of encroaching sand, which destroyed the fertility of the surrounding land and forced them to abandon the castle by the end of the 14th century.

Coastal pines fringe Caswell Bay

Caswell Bay & Pwlldu Bay

A splendid coastal walk exploring two beautiful bays, a smugglers' cove and a secluded wooded valley

What to expect:
Sandy beach, good-quality coast path, field and woodland paths

Distance/time: 7.5km/ 4¾ miles. Allow 3 hours

Start: Pay and Display car park at Caswell Bay

Grid ref: SS 593 876

Ordnance Survey Map: Explorer 164 Gower, *Llanelli*

After the walk: Beach cafés at Caswell Bay

Walk outline

From Caswell Bay, the walk follows an undulating coastal path past Brandy Cove to Pwlldu Bay. It then heads inland up the beautiful Bishopston Valley, the highlight of this section being the splendid viewpoint at Hanging Cliff. Field and woodland paths lead back to the coast, high above Pwlldu Bay. An elevated path, along the grassy cliff tops, returns to Brandy Cove, where the outward route is rejoined back to Caswell Bay.

Caswell Bay & Pwlldu Bay

These contrasting but equally beautiful bays encapsulate two different aspects of the Gower Peninsula. The first is represented by Caswell Bay, a popular sandy beach with lots of facilities. Tranquil Pwlldu Bay — accessible by cars only along a steep, stony track — provides the second.

Pwlldu National Trust sign

Behind Pwlldu Bay lies the Bishopston Valley, a deep wooded cleft in the south Gower coast. At one time, the valley would have been divided into fields by dry-stone walls; even today there are cleared areas of meadowland grazed by cattle. Higher up, the Bishopston Pill has carved an underground passage through pervious limestone. The stream reappears near the evocatively named Guzzle Hole.

Sea pinks, or 'thrift'

The Walk

1. From the car park, cross the road to the beach and turn right (to avoid wet feet, cross the stream where it emerges from a culvert). Follow the top of the beach to a corner in front of a large block of flats and join a narrow **flight of steps** climbing steeply up the side of the cliff. At the top of the steps, turn left, following a sign for 'Brandy Cove'.

For a short period at high tide the beach is impassable. When this is the case, follow the signed high tide route up the road to the right for some 600 metres. Take a private road on the left past a house called Delfan and continue onto a narrow path into woodland. The path hugs a fence above houses, rejoining the main route at the top of the steps from **Caswell Bay**.

As you leave Caswell Bay, the path rounds an exposed headland where an unprotected drop may make some walkers nervous. Beyond this point, the path winds gently along the coast to **Brandy Cove**.

As its name suggests, this small secluded bay was once used by smugglers. Besides brandy, gin, tea and tobacco were also landed illegally on the beach. Smugglers could land a cargo and disappear within minutes in the wooded valley.

From Brandy Cove, continue along the undulating coast path as far as **Pwlldu Bay** (a stone cross-path descending obliquely from the right can be used to access the beach). The main route continues to curve right, shortly reaching a T-junction with a stony track. Turn left downhill, following the sign for 'Pwlldu Bay'.

Emerge from beneath trees into an open grassy area with a **ford** ahead.

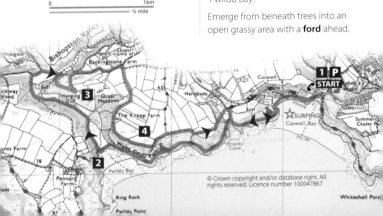

Subtropical heaven?: *Pines, roses and exotic plants clothe the cliffs above Caswell Bay*

Leave the track to the right, following a waymark across the grass to a **footbridge** over the stream. Once across, leave the coast path by turning right, signposted for 'Bishopston Valley'.

2. Follow the obvious path across thickly wooded slopes, above an area of marshland on the right. Once past the marshy area, the path drops to continue up the valley alongside a small river.

Where this bends right, bear left up steps and follow a twisting path uphill to a signed junction. Turn right here, down the slope, following a sign for 'Kittle and Bishopston'.

Rejoining the river, continue upstream, passing two paths on the left in quick succession. Just after the second path, turn right over a footbridge across the river, signed to 'Bishopston'. A short distance ahead, turn right off the main path to follow a yellow footpath waymark onto a narrow, stepped path climbing out of the valley. At a fork in a

Summer sands: *Caswell Bay's pristine 'Blue Flag' beach is popular with holidaymakers*

clearing, bear left to continue uphill with the embankment of an **Iron Age fort** to your right. Keep left at the top of the fort, along the clearer path up steps.

Some distance above the fort, a path joins your route from the left. Keep ahead to reach a bench and **viewpoint at Hanging Cliff**, where there is a spectacular vista down Bishopston Valley to Pwlldu Bay.

3. From the viewpoint, retrace your steps to where, on your upward route, a path joined from the left. Fork right

here and continue to a junction of paths beyond a kissing gate. Following a blue bridleway arrow, turn right and pass through a gate onto an enclosed track. Where the track joins a tarmac lane, bear left.

Just over 100 metres ahead, turn right through a waymarked kissing gate. Keep ahead along the right-hand edge of a field and follow the well-marked path through a series of metal kissing gates. Just past a white house on the left called 'The Knapp Farm', the path forks. Stay ahead on the upper, left-hand path, which soon emerges on a cliff overlooking **Pwlldu Bay**.

4. The obvious cliff-top path soon meets the vehicle access track to the bay. Turn left and then leave the track over a stile on the right. Keep ahead along another cliff-top path until a waymark directs you downhill to the left. Descend steeply on a stepped path through woodland and cross a field to reach a junction with a track. Turn right and follow the track down to **Brandy Cove**. Turning left onto the coast path, retrace your outward route back to **Caswell Bay**. ◆

Pwlldu Bay

Until 1902, Pwlldu Bay was the site of a busy limestone quarry employing over 200 people. Much of the stone produced was shipped across the Bristol Channel to Devon and Cornwall, where there was considerable demand for crushed limestone as an agricultural fertiliser. Quarrying was undoubtedly thirsty work — at one time there were no fewer than five popular pubs behind the bay!

Useful Information

Wales Coast Path

Comprehensive information about all sections of the Wales Coast Path can be found at: **www.walescoastpath.co.uk**

Visit Wales

The Visit Wales website covers everything from accommodation and events to attractions and adventure. For information on the area covered by this book, see the 'Carmarthenshire' and 'Swansea Bay, Mumbles and Gower' sections at: www. visitwales.co.uk

Tourist Information Centres

The main TICs provide free information on everything from accommodation and travel to what's on and walking advice.

Carmarthen	01267 231 557	carmarthentic@carmarthenshire.gov.uk
Llanelli	01554 777 744	discoverycentre@carmarthenshire.gov.uk
Mumbles	01792 361 302	info@mumblestic.co.uk
Swansea	01792 468 321	tourism@swansea.gov.uk

Travel

Information on public transport in Wales is available from Traveline Cymru. Call 0871 200 22 33 or visit **www.traveline-cymru.info**

Tide Times

Some of the walks in this book may be affected by tidal conditions. Tide tables for the coming week are available from: **www.bbc.co.uk/weather/coast_and_sea/tide_tables**. Tide tables are also available to buy from local TICs.

Weather

The Met Office operates a 24 hour online weather forecast. See **www.metoffice.gov.uk** for further details. Weather apps for a variety of smart phones are also available to download free of charge.